Rites on the Way

Church House Publishing

Published by   Church House Publishing
                      Church House
                      Great Smith Street
                      London SW1P 3AZ

Copyright ©   *The Archbishops' Council 2006*

                      First Published 2006
                      Second Impression 2013

                      978–0–7151–2209–9

Printed and bound by Core Publications Ltd, Kettering.

Typeset in Gill Sans by John Morgan Studio
Designed by John Morgan Studio

The material in this booklet is extracted from
Common Worship: Christian Initiation. It comprises:

¶   Rites Supporting Disciples on the Way to Christ
¶   Celebration after an Initiation Service outside the Parish
¶   Admission of the Baptized to Communion

For other material, page references to *Common Worship:
Christian Initiation* are supplied.

Pagination   This booklet has two sets of page numbers. The outer numbers
                    are the booklet's own page numbers, while the inner numbers
                    near the centre of most pages refer to the equivalent pages in
                    Common Worship: Christian Initiation.

Contents

¶ Authorization

The following material has been commended by the House of Bishops of the General Synod for use by the minister in exercise of his or her discretion under Canon B 5 of the Canons of the Church of England:

¶   Rites Supporting Disciples on the Way of Christ

¶   Celebration after an Initiation Service outside the Parish

¶   Admission of the Baptized to Communion

Rites Supporting Disciples on the Way of Christ

Contents

Notes

1 **Godparents and Sponsors**
The term 'godparent' is used for those asked to present children for baptism and to continue to support them. The term 'sponsor' is used for those who agree to offer support to candidates of any age for baptism, confirmation or affirmation of baptismal faith on their journey of faith. It is not necessary that a new disciple have the same person as godparent and sponsor. At the Welcome, the new disciple should agree with the minister on a member of the church to be their companion and supporter, and to act as their sponsor. A prayer is provided for the commissioning of godparents and sponsors within the Welcome of Those Preparing for the Baptism of Children (page 4) and the Welcome of Disciples on the Way of Faith (page 6).

2   **Testimony**
       The giving of a personal testimony in these rites or in an initiation
       service is to be encouraged. It is a public opportunity both for the
       new disciples to express their faith and for the Christian community
       to be encouraged and enthused to continue to spread the good
       news of God's kingdom. Such testimony will affirm the mission of
       the Church and allow the congregation to learn from the
       experience of the new disciples. It is important that testimony
       should be appropriate in length and style and not detract from the
       rest of the service. If a public act of testimony is not appropriate,
       a testimony may be given in written form.

3   **Giving of Gifts**
       It may be appropriate, particularly at the Welcome (pages 5–7)
       and the Thanksgiving for Holy Baptism (pages 32–35), to give
       the new disciple a gift to express the welcome and support of
       the church community. Depending on the recipient and the nature
       of the church community, a book, for example a prayer book, may
       be appropriate. However, in some communities a picture or icon,
       a cross, carving or sculpture or some other symbol of Christian
       faith may be a more suitable encouragement for the new disciple.

4   **The Giving of the Gospel and the Bible**
       The giving of a book of Scripture at services of commitment is
       encouraged. It is suggested that a Gospel is given at the Welcome
       of Those Preparing for the Baptism of Children (pages 3–4), if
       one has not already been given at a Thanksgiving for the Gift of a
       Child. A Gospel may also be given at the Call (pages 9–11), when
       it is expected that a new disciple will engage with the Bible, and
       particularly the life of Jesus, in church, in the group and in personal
       devotions. It may be appropriate to give a Bible at the Call, or leave
       the presentation of a Bible to the service of initiation, or to the
       Thanksgiving for Holy Baptism (pages 32–35), when the disciple
       moves into a new relationship with Christ and the Church.

¶ Welcome of Those Preparing for the Baptism of Children

Note

This rite may be used during baptism preparation, or as part of the Sunday service when the child is first brought to church. If it is to be used within a celebration of Holy Communion, it may be used before the prayers of intercession, at the peace, or before the dismissal. It may also be appropriate to invite godparents and sponsors to be present; they may be commissioned during this rite. If a Gospel has not been given at a service of Thanksgiving for the Gift of a Child (*Common Worship: Christian Initiation*, pages 16–28) it may be appropriate to give one on this occasion.

Welcome

The minister may address the congregation

Today we welcome *N and N, and N and N*, who are preparing for the baptism of their *children N and N*. As the people of God in this place, will you welcome *these children* and support *their families* by your prayers and fellowship as they prepare for *their children's* baptism?

All **With the help of God, we will.**

A large candle is lit.

The minister may ask the parents, godparents and sponsors to come forward with their children and says, in these or other suitable words

We thank God for his presence in your *lives*
and for the grace that has brought you here today.

Baptism is the sign of new life in Christ. You share with us the responsibility for encouraging *these children* in the new life that Jesus Christ offers to us all. Will you pray for *these children,* and help *them* to grow in the knowledge and love of God and to take *their* place in the life and worship of the Church?
With the help of God, we will.

Eternal and loving God,
you have promised that those who seek will find you;
we pray for your blessing on *these families*
as they prepare for the baptism of *N and N,*
that they may walk together in the Way of Christ.
By your grace, may *N and N* become your *children*
and take *their* place within the community of your Church,
through Jesus Christ our Lord.

All   **Amen.**

The minister may introduce and commission the godparents and
sponsors using these or other suitable words

N and N, you have been asked to nurture *these children* as *they*
grow in faith.

May God bring you joy as you hold *them* in his love,
and walk with *them* on the Way of Christ.
May you be a blessing to one another,
and may the blessing of God almighty,
the Father, the Son and the Holy Spirit,
be among you and remain with you always. Amen.

¶ *Welcome of Disciples on the Way of Faith*

Notes

1   This rite is intended for those who, after an initial exploration of the Christian faith, wish to learn the Christian Way within the life of the people of God. It is not intended for initial enquirers, but for those who want to commit themselves to continuing the journey of faith. One or more members of the Church should be invited to be the companion(s) of each new disciple, and to act as their sponsors. Those sponsors may be commissioned during this rite.

2   The Welcome should be included in an act of public worship, and may be used before the collect, after the sermon or before the peace. The rite might begin outside the church building or at the church door, where the new disciples are welcomed by the Christian community, and particularly by their sponsors, and accompanied into the church in procession.

3   It may be appropriate to give the new disciple a gift to express the welcome and support of the church community (see Note 3 on page 2).

Welcome

The minister may introduce the Welcome in these or similar words

Today it is our joy and privilege to welcome *N and N* as *disciples* on the Way of Christ. *They* are among us as a sign of the journey of faith to which we are all called.

The minister invites the disciples to stand before the people with their sponsors. The sponsors introduce them, and the minister says

We thank God for his presence in your *lives*
and for the grace that has brought you here today.
We welcome you.

What is it that you seek?

The disciples may reply in their own words, or may say

To learn the Way of Christ.

The minister addresses the congregation

We welcome N *and* N
in the love and hope of Christ.
Will you support and pray for *them,*
and learn with *them* the Way of Christ?

All   **With the help of God, we will.**

*The minister may introduce the sponsors and address them using these
or other suitable words*

Will you accompany N *and* N on the journey of faith,
supporting *them* with friendship, love and prayer?
With the help of God, we will.

*The minister may commission the sponsors using these
or other suitable words*

May God give you the gift of love
to serve N *and* N whom he loved first.
May God give you the gift of faith
to share the good news of his kingdom.
May God give you the gift of joy
as you journey together with Jesus our Lord.
And may the blessing of God almighty,
the Father, the Son and the Holy Spirit,
be among you and remain with you always. Amen.

*The minister then addresses each candidate separately
or the group together*

Will you receive the sign of the cross,
as a mark of Christ's love for you as you explore his Way?
I will.

*The minister makes the sign of the cross on the forehead of each
candidate. The sponsors may be invited to sign the candidates with the
cross. The minister says*

Receive the sign of the cross.
May Christ our Redeemer,
who claims you for his own,
deliver you from evil and guide you on the Way.

Where a candidate is already baptized, the minister uses these words

Receive the sign of the cross.
May Christ our Redeemer,
who in your baptism claimed you for his own,
protect and guide you.

Prayer may be offered for each new disciple. After all have been prayed with, the minister says this or a similar prayer. It may be said over each disciple or the whole group.

God of life,
you give us the gift of faith.
Guide *N and N* by your wisdom
and surround *them* with your love.
Deepen *their* knowledge of Christ
and set *their* feet on the Way that leads to life.
May your people uphold *them* in love,
find in *them* a sign of hope,
and learn with *them* the Way of Christ.

All **Amen.**

A gift expressing welcome to the new disciple from the congregation may be given.

¶ *Affirmation of the Christian Way*

Note

This may be used in public worship when special significance
is being given to the presence of disciples on the Way, for example
at the Welcome or the Call. It may also be suitable in informal
settings as an introduction or reminder about the shape of the
Way. Where appropriate, it may be led by two or three people.

Affirmation of the Christian Way

As we follow the Way of Christ,
we affirm the presence of God among us,
Father, Son and Holy Spirit.

God calls us to share in worship.
Jesus said, where two or three are gathered in my name,
I am there among them.

All **Jesus, you are the Way: guide us on our journey.**

God calls us to share in prayer.
Jesus said, remain in me, and I will remain in you.

All **Jesus, you are the Way: guide us on our journey.**

God calls us to share the Scriptures.
Jesus met his disciples on the road
and opened the Scriptures to them.

All **Jesus, you are the Way: guide us on our journey.**

God calls us to share in communion.
Jesus said, do this in remembrance of me.

All **Jesus, you are the Way: guide us on our journey.**

God calls us to share in service.
Jesus said, as you do it for the least of these, you do it for me.

All **Jesus, you are the Way: guide us on our journey.**

God calls us to share the good news.
Jesus said, go and make disciples of all nations.

All **Jesus, you are the Way: guide us on our journey.**

¶ *Call and Celebration of the Decision to be Baptized or Confirmed or to Affirm Baptismal Faith*

Notes

1   The Call is intended for those who wish to continue on the Way, following a period of exploration and regular involvement in the Christian community.

2   The Call should be included in an act of public worship, and may be used before the collect, after the sermon or before the peace.

3   At the Signing with the Cross, a priest may anoint the candidate with pure olive oil, reflecting the practice of athletes preparing for a contest. It is appropriate that the oil should be that consecrated by the bishop for Signing with the Cross. If oil is used, care should be taken that the candidates understand the symbolism and significance of anointing (see *Common Worship: Christian Initiation*, pages 345–346). When a candidate for baptism is anointed during the Call, oil is not used for the Signing with the Cross in Baptism; however, oil mixed with fragrant spices (traditionally called chrism), expressing the blessings of the messianic era and the richness of the Holy Spirit, is used to accompany the prayer after the baptism, if it is not to be used at confirmation.

4   Where a disciple has already been baptized, the second form is used at the Signing with the Cross.

Call and Celebration

The minister may introduce the Call in these or similar words

Today it is our joy and privilege to welcome *N and N*,
disciples with us on the Way of Christ.
They are among us as a sign of the journey of faith to which we
are all called.

The minister invites the disciples to stand before the people with their
sponsors. The disciples are presented to the congregation by their
sponsors, and some words of personal commendation may be said.
The minister says

We thank God for his presence in your *lives*
and for the grace that has brought you here today.

What is it that you seek?

The disciples may reply in their own words, or may say

To follow the Way of Christ.

The minister may ask the sponsors to confirm the candidates'
commitment to worship, prayer and the fellowship of the Church,
and their readiness to study and to understand their story as part
of the people of God. The names of those who seek initiation may
be added to a book dedicated for that purpose.

The minister then addresses each candidate separately or the
group together

Will you receive the sign of the cross
as a mark of Christ's love for you
as you explore his Way?
I will.

The minister makes the sign of the cross on the forehead of each
candidate. The sponsors may be invited to sign the candidates with the
cross. The minister says

Receive the sign of the cross.
May Christ our Redeemer,
who claims you for his own,
deliver you from evil and guide you on the Way.

Where a candidate is already baptized, the minister uses these words

Receive the sign of the cross.
May Christ our Redeemer,
who in your baptism claimed you for his own,
protect and guide you.

A copy of a Gospel is presented, with these words

Receive this book.
It is the good news of God's love.
Take it as your guide.

The candidates remain in front of the congregation for the prayers of intercession. This or other similar forms may be used (see pages 25–27).

N and N, who are our brothers and sisters, have already travelled a long road. We rejoice with *them* in the gentle guidance of God. Let us pray that *they* may press onwards, until *they* come to share fully in the Way of Christ.

May God the Father reveal his Christ to *them* more and more with every passing day.
Lord, in your mercy

All　**hear our prayer.**

May *they* undertake with generous *hearts* and *souls* whatever God may ask of *them*.
Lord, in your mercy

All　**hear our prayer.**

May *they* have our sincere and unfailing support every step of the way.
Lord, in your mercy

All　**hear our prayer.**

May *their hearts* and ours become more responsive to the needs of others.
Lord, in your mercy

All　**hear our prayer.**

In due time may *they* come *to baptism I to confirmation I to reaffirm their baptismal faith,* and receive the renewal of the Holy Spirit.
Lord, in your mercy

All　**hear our prayer.**

¶ *The Presentation of the Four Texts*

Note

In order to give shape to their discipleship, all baptized Christians should be encouraged to explore these four texts and make them their own: the Summary of the Law, the Lord's Prayer, the Apostles' Creed, and the Beatitudes. The texts may be presented on cards or found in personal Bibles, either within a study group or in public worship, possibly after the sermon.

Jesus' Summary of the Law

One of the following or other readings may be used

Exodus 20.1-19; Leviticus 19.9-18; Romans 8.1-4; Romans 13.8-10;
Galatians 5.13, 14; Mark 12.28-34

One of the following psalms may be used

Psalm 1; 15; 119.9-16; 119.97-104

The minister addresses those who are disciples on the Way of faith

Brothers and sisters, listen carefully to the words that Jesus gave us
as a summary of the law. These few words help us understand how
we are to live as human beings in God's world. They are given not to
condemn us but to show how by the grace of God we may live as
free people reflecting the goodness and love of God.

The Summary of the Law is read

Our Lord Jesus Christ said:
The first commandment is this:
'Hear, O Israel, the Lord our God is the only Lord.
You shall love the Lord your God with all your heart,
with all your soul, with all your mind,
and with all your strength.'

The second is this: 'Love your neighbour as yourself.'
There is no other commandment greater than these.
On these two commandments hang all the law and the prophets.

God of truth,
help us to keep your law of love
and to walk in ways of wisdom,
that we may find true life
in Jesus Christ your Son.

All **Amen.**

The Lord's Prayer

One of the following or other readings may be used

I Kings 8.27-30; Hosea 11.1-4; Romans 8.14-17, 26, 27;
Galatians 4.4-7; Matthew 6.7-13; Luke 11.1-4

One of the following psalms may be used

Psalm 23; 103.6-18

The minister addresses those who are disciples on the Way of faith

Brothers and sisters, listen carefully to the Lord's Prayer. It is given
to us as a pattern for our praying as well as a prayer that we can
make our own. It teaches us that heaven is open to our prayers
and that the world is open to the gracious working of God.

*The Lord's Prayer is read in the form which is commonly used by
the congregation.*

Our Father in heaven,
hallowed be your name,
your kingdom come,
your will be done,
on earth as in heaven.
Give us today our daily bread.
Forgive us our sins
as we forgive those who sin against us.
Lead us not into temptation
but deliver us from evil.
For the kingdom, the power,
and the glory are yours
now and for ever.
Amen.

(or)

Our Father, who art in heaven,
hallowed be thy name;
thy kingdom come;
thy will be done;
on earth as it is in heaven.
Give us this day our daily bread.
And forgive us our trespasses,
as we forgive those who trespass against us.
And lead us not into temptation;
but deliver us from evil.
For thine is the kingdom,
the power and the glory,
for ever and ever.
Amen.

The minister says

Lord of heaven and earth,
as Jesus taught his disciples to be persistent in prayer,
give us patience and courage never to lose hope,
but always to bring our prayers before you;
through Jesus Christ our Lord.

All **Amen.**

The Apostles' Creed

One of the following or other readings may be used

Deuteronomy 6.1-7; Deuteronomy 26.1-10; Romans 10.8-13;
1 Timothy 6.11-16; 2 Timothy 1.8-14; Matthew 16.13-18;
John 12.44-50

One of the following psalms may be used

Psalm 78. 1-7; 145.1-9

The minister addresses those who are disciples on the Way of faith

Brothers and sisters, listen carefully to this declaration of faith,
which the Church calls the Apostles' Creed. Christians have said
this together since the earliest centuries, especially at baptism,
where we confess that Jesus is our Lord and Saviour. It speaks of our
belief in God's love for the world, in creation, in incarnation and in
salvation.

The Apostles' Creed is read

I believe in God, the Father almighty,
creator of heaven and earth.

I believe in Jesus Christ, his only Son, our Lord,
who was conceived by the Holy Spirit,
born of the Virgin Mary,
suffered under Pontius Pilate,
was crucified, died, and was buried;
he descended to the dead.
On the third day he rose again;
he ascended into heaven,
he is seated at the right hand of the Father,
and he will come to judge the living and the dead.

I believe in the Holy Spirit,
the holy catholic Church,
the communion of saints,
the forgiveness of sins,
the resurrection of the body,
and the life everlasting.
Amen.

The minister says

Holy God,
faithful and unchanging:
enlarge our minds with the knowledge of your truth,
and draw us more deeply into the mystery of your love,
that we may truly worship you,
Father, Son and Holy Spirit,
one God, now and for ever.

All   **Amen.**

The Beatitudes – Blessings of the Gospel

One of the following or other readings may be used

Isaiah 2.2-4; Isaiah 11.1-10; Ephesians 3.7-13; 2 Corinthians 8.9;
1 John 3.1-3; Revelation 21.22-27; Mark 4.30-32

One of the following psalms may be used

Psalm 72.1-14; 87; 122

The minister addresses those who are disciples on the Way of faith

Brothers and sisters, listen carefully to these words from Jesus'
Sermon on the Mount. In them he declares the blessings of God's
kingdom. He gives us a vision of a world redeemed by love, and the
qualities of discipleship which will bring about that transformation.

The Beatitudes are read from either Matthew 5.3-10 or Luke 6.20-23

Matthew 5.3-10

Blessed are the poor in spirit,
for theirs is the kingdom of heaven.

Blessed are those who mourn,
for they shall be comforted.

Blessed are the meek,
for they shall inherit the earth.

Blessed are those who hunger and thirst after righteousness,
for they shall be satisfied.

Blessed are the merciful,
for they shall obtain mercy.

Blessed are the pure in heart,
for they shall see God.

Blessed are the peacemakers,
for they shall be called children of God.

Blessed are those who suffer persecution for righteousness' sake,
for theirs is the kingdom of heaven.

(or)

Luke 6.20-23

Blessed are you who are poor,
for yours is the kingdom of God.

Blessed are you who are hungry now,
for you will be filled.

Blessed are you who weep now,
for you will laugh.

Blessed are you when people hate you,
and when they exclude you, revile you,
and defame you on account of the Son of Man.

Rejoice in that day and leap for joy,
for surely your reward is great in heaven;
for that is what their ancestors did to the prophets.

The minister says

Almighty God,
you search us and know us:
may we rely on you in strength
and rest on you in weakness,
now and in all our days;
through Jesus Christ our Lord.

All　**Amen.**

Note
These prayers may be used as part of baptism preparation, within
a study group, or on the evening before the baptism either at home
or in church.

Prayers in Preparation for Baptism

Candles may be lit.

Blessed are you, sovereign God of all;
you lead us from death to life.
In baptism you create a new people,
cleansing us from sin,
consecrating us to service,
and transferring us from the dominion of darkness
into the kingdom of your beloved Son,
where with all your people, we may know your grace
and proclaim your unchanging glory.
Blessed be God, Father, Son and Holy Spirit.

All   **Blessed be God for ever.**

*Two or three short readings may be read, interspersed with silence or
appropriate music. The readings may be drawn from those of the season
or may reflect the particular circumstances of the candidates and their
families. Other possible readings include*

Matthew 3.13- 4.2; Mark 1.1-8; John 3.1-6; Romans 6.3-5;
Romans 8.14-17; Colossians 1.9-14; Colossians 3.1-14; 1 Peter 1.3-9

A period of reflection and prayer follows.

The Lord who called us has called us by name.

All   **Father of all, renew us and bring us life.**

The Lord who formed us has also redeemed us.

All   **Jesus, light of the world, love us and bring us life.**

When we pass through fire and water, the Lord will be with us.

All   **Spirit of God, lead us and bring us life.**

We shall not be overwhelmed,
for the Lord God is our saviour.

All   **Creator, redeemer, sustainer, bring us life. Amen.**

(or)

Lord God, in the beginning you called forth light
to dispel the darkness that lay upon the face of the deep.
Deliver your servants from the powers of evil
and enlighten us with your presence,
that with open eyes and glad hearts
we may worship you and serve you,
now and for ever.

All **Amen.**

Lord Christ, true light of the world,
shine, we pray, in the hearts of your people,
that we might see the Way that leads to eternal life,
and follow without stumbling;
for you are the Way, O Christ,
as you are the Truth and the Life.

All **Amen.**

Come, Holy Spirit, come;
come as wind, come as fire.
Convict, convert and consecrate our hearts and minds,
to our great good, and to your great glory;
who with the Father and the Son are one God,
now and for ever.

All **Amen.**

The people may be invited to add their own prayers.

The Lord's Prayer is said (see page 29).

The prayers conclude with

Gracious God,
whose faithfulness never fails,
may those who seek find the kingdom,
those who knock see an opened door,
those who ask receive the gift of new life
which you offer freely to all
in Jesus Christ.

All **Amen.**

Let us bless the Lord.

All **Thanks be to God.**

Resources

Being welcomed as a disciple begins a journey of exploration of the Christian Way; central to that journey is regular reflection in a group that explores different aspects of Christianity. The disciple may meet with a group during the week, perhaps following a course, or a group may leave the regular congregation during the normal service before the sermon. It is important that the congregation prays regularly for those exploring the Christian Way and is encouraged to see them as models of Christian learning.

New disciples should be helped and encouraged into a daily, sustaining discipline of prayer and reflection on Scripture. Therefore, it may be appropriate for a regular group to use Prayer during the Day or Morning or Evening Prayer from *Common Worship: Daily Prayer*. At the appropriate time either might include the Presentation of the Four Texts (pages 12–19).

¶ Traditional Prayers for Use with Learning Groups

These traditional prayers are taken from Prayer During the Day.

Christ be with me, Christ within me,
Christ behind me, Christ before me,
Christ beside me, Christ to win me,
Christ to comfort and restore me,
Christ beneath me, Christ above me,
Christ in quiet, Christ in danger,
Christ in hearts of all that love me,
Christ in mouth of friend and stranger. *from St Patrick's Breastplate*

Eternal God,
the light of the minds that know you,
the joy of the hearts that love you,
and the strength of the wills that serve you:
grant us so to know you
that we may truly love you,
so to love you that we may truly serve you,
whose service is perfect freedom;
through Jesus Christ our Lord. *after Augustine of Hippo (430)*

Eternal light, shine into our hearts,
eternal goodness, deliver us from evil,
eternal power, be our support,
eternal wisdom, scatter the darkness of our ignorance,
eternal pity, have mercy upon us;
that with all our heart and mind and soul and strength
we may seek your face and be brought by your infinite mercy
    to your holy presence,
through Jesus Christ our Lord. *Alcuin of York (804)*

God be in my head, and in my understanding;
God be in my eyes, and in my looking;
God be in my mouth, and in my speaking;
God be in my heart, and in my thinking;
God be at mine end, and at my departing. *Sarum Primer*

Lord Jesus Christ, we thank you
for all the benefits you have won for us,
for all the pains and insults you have borne for us.
Most merciful redeemer,
friend and brother,
may we know you more clearly,
love you more dearly,
and follow you more nearly,
day by day.   *after Richard of Chichester (1253)*

O gracious and holy Father,
give us wisdom to perceive you,
diligence to seek you,
patience to wait for you,
eyes to behold you,
a heart to meditate upon you,
and a life to proclaim you,
through the power of the Spirit
of Jesus Christ our Lord.   *Benedict of Nursia (c. 550)*

O Lord our God,
grant us grace to desire you with our whole heart;
that so desiring, we may seek and find you;
and so finding, may love you;
and so loving, may hate those sins from which
    you have delivered us;
through Jesus Christ our Lord.   *Anselm (1109)*

A prayer before Bible reading

O Lord, you have given us your word
for a light to shine upon our path.
Grant us so to meditate on that word,
and to follow its teaching,
that we may find in it the light
that shines more and more until the perfect day;
through Jesus Christ our Lord.   *after Jerome (420)*

¶ *Prayers of Intercession*

In the power of the Spirit let us pray to the Father,
through Jesus Christ who is the Way, the Truth and the Life.

We pray for all who follow the Way of Christ
and for the unity of all Christian people;
break down that which separates us from one another and from you,
that knowing your forgiveness we may share your love
   with a needy world.
Lord, hear us.

All   **Lord, graciously hear us.**

We pray for those who hold positions of responsibility and power
both internationally and in our local communities;
may your Holy Spirit guide them in their decision-making,
so that paths of truth and justice may be open to everyone.
Lord, hear us.

All   **Lord, graciously hear us.**

We give you thanks and pray
for all who support and care for us as we follow the Way of Christ,
our families and friends,
and our fellow pilgrims along the way;
nourish us all with the words of life and the bread of heaven,
that we may worship you joyfully,
listen to you willingly
and serve you gladly.
Lord, hear us.

All   **Lord, graciously hear us.**

We pray for those who,
through sickness, misfortune or abuse,
feel that their lives are without meaning or direction;
surround them with your love,
and give wisdom and patience to all who support and guide them.
Lord, hear us.

All   **Lord, graciously hear us.**

We thank you for the fullness of life you give us in Jesus Christ,
and for all whose lives have been an example of your truth
    and life for us;
may our communion with them, and with all the saints,
nourish and support us on our earthly pilgrimage.
Lord, hear us.

All   **Lord, graciously hear us.**

(or)

Surround with your love those exploring the Way of Christ
and set their feet on the way that leads to life.
May your people learn with them the Way of Christ
and find in them a sign of hope.
Lord, in your mercy

All   **hear our prayer.**

Guide with your wisdom
those who have heard the call to seek the way of life
and deepen their knowledge and love of Christ.
Lord, in your mercy

All   **hear our prayer.**

Give your grace to those whom we have welcomed
as learners in the Way of Christ
and grant them the wisdom that leads to life in Christ.
Lord, in your mercy

All   **hear our prayer.**

Support with your grace and protection
all who have set themselves to learn the Way of Christ,
that they may know your love
and be a source of life to others.
Lord, in your mercy

All   **hear our prayer.**

(or)

God of all time and space, one God in Trinity,
turn your ear to hear us as we pray.
Hear us, Lord.

All   **Hear us, Lord, and all your pilgrim Church.**

Guiding Israel with fire and cloud,
you led your chosen people from captivity to the promised land.
We pray for guidance as we search out the Way,
and wisdom for those struggling to find it.
Guide us, Lord.

All **Guide us, Lord, and all your pilgrim Church.**

Revealed in burning bush and in mountain cloud,
you gave the law, and taught your people.
We ask that, learning from the Scriptures,
we may grow in love for you and for one another.
Teach us, Lord.

All **Teach us, Lord, and all your pilgrim Church.**

Father, you sent your Son in human frailty;
in the garden, he accepted the cup of death.
We pray for strength to meet the challenges before us,
and remember those who have inspired your Church to faith ...
Strengthen us, Lord.

All **Strengthen us, Lord, and all your pilgrim Church.**

Jesus, healer of the sick,
worker of miracles, friend of the outcast;
we ask for grace to care
for our neighbours throughout the world;
especially we pray for ...
Sustain us, Lord.

All **Sustain us, Lord, and all your pilgrim Church.**

Holy Spirit, living breath of living God,
you inspired the apostles to preach good news.
Help us to bear witness to your love
with cheerful hearts and constant courage.
Inspire us, Lord.

All **Inspire us, Lord, and all your pilgrim Church.**

Loving Father of all creation,
loving Saviour in form of a servant,
loving Spirit, present among us,
God of all time and space, one God in Trinity,
we offer up our prayers to you.
Hear us, Lord.

All **Hear us, Lord, and all your pilgrim Church.**

¶ ## At the Preparation of the Table

Adults, young people and children may bring forward the gifts and help with the preparation of the table. They then lead the congregation in the prayer at the preparation of the table.

With this bread that we bring
All **we shall remember Jesus.**

With this wine that we bring
All **we shall remember Jesus.**

Bread for his body,
wine for his blood,
gifts from God to his table we bring.
All **We shall remember Jesus.**

¶ ## At the Dismissal

Adults, young people and children may lead the following

To a troubled world
peace from Christ.
To a searching world
love from Christ.
To a waiting world
hope from Christ.

¶ ## At the Giving of a Bible

Receive this Bible.
Hear God's word with us.
Learn and tell its stories.
Rejoice in its good news.
Discover its mysteries.
Honour its commandments.
May God's life-giving word be sweeter to you than honey
and lead you in the Way of Christ.

¶ *The Lord's Prayer*

As our Saviour taught us, so we pray

All **Our Father in heaven,
hallowed be your name,
your kingdom come,
your will be done,
on earth as in heaven.
Give us today our daily bread.
Forgive us our sins
as we forgive those who sin against us.
Lead us not into temptation
but deliver us from evil.
For the kingdom, the power,
and the glory are yours
now and for ever.
Amen.**

(or)

Let us pray with confidence as our Saviour has taught us

All **Our Father, who art in heaven,
hallowed be thy name;
thy kingdom come;
thy will be done;
on earth as it is in heaven.
Give us this day our daily bread.
And forgive us our trespasses,
as we forgive those who trespass against us.
And lead us not into temptation;
but deliver us from evil.
For thine is the kingdom,
the power and the glory,
for ever and ever.
Amen.**

Celebration after an Initiation Service outside the Parish

Note

When baptism, confirmation and/or affirmation of baptismal faith have been celebrated outside the parish, for example in the cathedral church or in another church within the deanery, it may be appropriate for the regular congregation to acknowledge this important transition. If this Celebration is used, it should normally be included in the principal service on the following Sunday.

Pastoral Introduction

This may be read by those present before the service begins.

Baptism marks the beginning of a journey with God which continues for the rest of our lives. In the last *months N and N* have been exploring the meaning of baptism in Jesus Christ. They have looked together at the call to discipleship in the world and in the Church. They have sought to understand the responsibilities of discipleship in today's world. We celebrate with them their baptism / confirmation by Bishop N / affirmation of baptismal faith and will seek to learn with them the Way of Christ.

Prayers of Intercession

At the Prayers of Intercession the following may be used

We pray for N and N,
that they may continue to grow in the grace of Christ,
take their place among the company of your people,
and reflect your glory in the world.
Lord, in your mercy

All **hear our prayer.**

The Welcome and Peace

The president says

I present to you *N and N* who have recently been baptized /
confirmed / affirmed their baptismal faith. Will you welcome them
and uphold them in their new life in Christ?

All   **With the help of God, we will.**

There is one Lord, one faith, one baptism:
N and N, by one Spirit we are all baptized into one body.

All   **We welcome you into the fellowship of faith;**
we are children of the same heavenly Father;
we welcome you.

An opportunity may be given for testimony.

The president introduces the Peace in these or other suitable words

We are all one in Christ Jesus.
We belong to him through faith,
heirs of the promise of the Spirit of peace.

The peace of the Lord be always with you
All   **and also with you.**

A minister may say
Let us offer one another a sign of peace.

All may exchange a sign of peace.

Thanksgiving for Holy Baptism

Notes

1   Thanksgiving for Holy Baptism should be made by the newly initiated and the regular congregation some weeks after initiation. This rite is based upon the general Thanksgiving for Holy Baptism (*Common Worship: Services and Prayers for the Church of England*, pages 48–49). It may instead be appropriate to use the Thanksgiving for the Mission of the Church (*Common Worship: Services and Prayers for the Church of England*, pages 54–56).

2   It may be appropriate to present the newly initiated with a gift during this rite. This may be a Bible if one has not already been given (see Note 4, page 2) or another gift.

This prayer of thanksgiving is said and water may be poured into the font

God in Christ gives us water welling up for eternal life.
With joy you will draw water from the wells of salvation.

All   **Lord, give us this water and we shall thirst no more.**

Let us give thanks to the Lord our God.

All   **It is right to give thanks and praise.**

Blessed are you, sovereign God of all,
to you be glory and praise for ever.
You are our light and our salvation.
From the deep waters of death
you have raised your Son to life in triumph.
Grant that all who have been born anew by water and the Spirit
may daily be renewed in your image,
walk by the light of faith,
and serve you in newness of life;
through your anointed Son, Jesus Christ,
to whom with you and the Holy Spirit
we lift our voices of praise.
Blessed be God, Father, Son and Holy Spirit.

All   **Blessed be God for ever.**

The minister leads the congregation in the Commission

Those who are baptized are called to worship and serve God.

Will you continue in the apostles' teaching and fellowship,
in the breaking of bread, and in the prayers?

All   **With the help of God, I will.**

Will you persevere in resisting evil,
and, whenever you fall into sin, repent and return to the Lord?

All   **With the help of God, I will.**

Will you proclaim by word and example
the good news of God in Christ?

All   **With the help of God, I will.**

Will you seek and serve Christ in all people,
loving your neighbour as yourself?

All   **With the help of God, I will.**

Will you acknowledge Christ's authority over human society,
by prayer for the world and its leaders,
by defending the weak, and by seeking peace and justice?

All   **With the help of God, I will.**

Eternal God, our beginning and our end,
preserve in your people the new life of baptism;
as Christ receives us on earth,
so may he guide us through the trials of this world
and enfold us in the joy of heaven,
where you live and reign,
one God for ever and ever.

All   **Amen.**

Those who have recently been baptized or confirmed, or have recently affirmed their baptismal faith, may be invited forward. They may be given the opportunity to give testimony, and may then be presented with a gift.

Prayers of intercession are offered. These should include prayer for those who are preparing for baptism and for those recently baptized. They may end with this or another collect

Almighty God,
in our baptism you have consecrated us
to be temples of your Holy Spirit.
May we, whom you have counted worthy,
nurture this gift of your indwelling Spirit with a lively faith
and worship you with upright lives;
through Jesus Christ our Lord.

All **Amen.**

The water may be sprinkled over the people or they may be invited to sign themselves with the cross using the water in the font. The minister says

As we follow the Way of Christ,
we affirm the presence of God among us,
Father, Son and Holy Spirit.

(The words in italics may be spoken by a second voice.)

God calls us to share in worship.
*Jesus said, where two or three are gathered in my name,
I am there among them.*

All **Jesus, you are the Way: guide us on our journey.**

God calls us to share in prayer.
Jesus said, remain in me, and I will remain in you.

All **Jesus, you are the Way: guide us on our journey.**

God calls us to share the Scriptures.
*Jesus met his disciples on the road
and opened the Scriptures to them.*

All **Jesus, you are the Way: guide us on our journey.**

God calls us to share in communion.
Jesus said, do this in remembrance of me.

All **Jesus, you are the Way: guide us on our journey.**

God calls us to share in service.
Jesus said, as you do it for the least of these, you do it for me.

All **Jesus, you are the Way: guide us on our journey.**

God calls us to share the good news.
Jesus said, go and make disciples of all nations.

All **Jesus, you are the Way: guide us on our journey.**

The service ends either with the Peace or with the following blessing said from the font

May God, who in Christ gives us a spring of water
   welling up to eternal life,
perfect in *you* the image of his glory;
and the blessing of God almighty,
the Father, the Son, and the Holy Spirit,
be among *you* and remain with *you* always.

All **Amen.**

Admission of the Baptized to Communion

Notes

1 This rite is intended for use in accordance with any regulations made by the General Synod under Canon B 15A.

2 The congregation should be made aware that people from the church are being prepared for communion. Those being prepared can be introduced to the congregation, for example by displaying photographs (with consent) and by inviting the congregation to pray for them. Godparents and sponsors, as well as families, may be invited to the service. In the case of children, the goodwill of those parents who are not regularly members of the congregation should always be sought and obtained.

3 To make it clear that the admission of the baptized to communion before confirmation is neither another baptism service nor a confirmation, baptismal water should not be used, and neither the laying on of hands nor anointing with oil should take place. Similarly, a bishop should not normally preside at this rite, as this might confuse it with confirmation. Those admitted should generally receive communion with their family and friends.

4 The rite should normally be used in a main Sunday service. It is not necessary to use every part of the order provided.

5 The Welcome of those being admitted may be used at the Greeting or before the Peace. If thought appropriate, the Questions may be used instead of the Welcome; if so, they are used before the Peace.

6 The Profession of Faith from the baptism service, the Affirmation of the Christian Way (page 8) and the forms of intercession on pages 25–27 may be particularly suitable.

Pastoral Introduction

This may be read by those present before the service begins.

Today we welcome to communion *N and N* who share faithfully and regularly in our worship. A person is admitted to communion on the basis of their baptism, the sign and pledge of incorporation into the death and resurrection of Christ and the new life of the kingdom of God. *N and N* have been baptized, and today they receive the sacrament of the body and blood of Christ with us. They are taking a new step in the life to which God has called them in baptism and which we trust they will later affirm in confirmation. We welcome them and look forward to learning with and from them as we journey together on the Way of Christ.

The Welcome

The president may invite those to be welcomed to stand before the people, and introduces them in these or other suitable words

We are God's pilgrim people.
We share in the story of God's love for the world,
God's love in Christ, calling us to himself,
God's love in the Spirit, giving strength for our journey of faith.
We celebrate this love in word and song,
we feed on Jesus in bread and wine
and make him known through our life together.

As the people of God in this place, we share the responsibility of encouraging one another in our worship and supporting one another in our discipleship, by our example and our prayers.

N and N, we welcome you in Jesus' name to receive communion with us.

At the Prayers of Intercession

We pray for *N and N*,
that they may draw near with confidence to your throne of grace
and know in their lives the transforming power of your love.
Lord, in your mercy

All **hear our prayer.**

The Peace

The president introduces the Peace in these or other suitable words

We are the body of Christ.
In the one Spirit we were all baptized into one body.
Let us then pursue all that makes for peace
and builds up our common life.

(or)

We are all one in Christ Jesus.
We belong to him through faith,
heirs of the promise of the Spirit of peace.

The peace of the Lord be always with you
All **and also with you.**

At the Preparation of the Table

Those welcomed to communion may lead the prayers at the preparation of the table.

With this bread that we bring
All **we shall remember Jesus.**

With this wine that we bring
All **we shall remember Jesus.**

Bread for his body,
wine for his blood,
gifts from God to his table we bring.
All **We shall remember Jesus.**

Proper Preface

And now we give you thanks
that you call us into the communion of your love;
your overflowing grace makes us partakers in the divine nature
and a sign of your kingdom.

Post Communion

The Post Communion of the day or this Post Communion is said

We praise and thank you, O Christ, for this sacred feast:
for here we receive you,
here the memory of your passion is renewed,
here our minds are filled with grace,
and here a pledge of future glory is given,
when we shall feast at that table where you reign
with all your saints for ever.

All   **Amen.**

At the Dismissal

*At the Dismissal, a blessing appropriate to the day or the blessing for the
Day of Pentecost (*Common Worship: Services and Prayers for the
Church of England, *page 321) may be used.*

*Those admitted to communion may be invited forward,
and the following may be said*

God has touched us with his love
and nourished us at his table.
As God's pilgrim people,
may we continue to explore the Way of Christ,
and grow in friendship with God,
in love for his people, and in serving others.

Those who have been admitted to communion may lead the following

To a troubled world
peace from Christ.

To a searching world
love from Christ.

To a waiting world
hope from Christ.

The Questions

If it is thought appropriate to use these Questions instead of the Welcome, they may be used before the Peace.

The minister addresses the congregation

Brothers and sisters, today we are welcoming *N and N* to Holy Communion. As parents and godparents, and as the community of *St N's*, we share the responsibility of encouraging them in their worship, and of supporting them by our friendship, our example and our prayers. Will you help them to grow in faith and love?

All   **We will.**

The minister addresses those being welcomed

N and N, you love God, you follow Jesus, and you live the Christian life. Do you wish to receive Holy Communion?
Yes.

As *N and N* receive today the sacrament of the body and blood of Christ, let us pray that we may all know and reflect the love of Christ.

God of life,
you invite us to eat at your table;
may we know your love
as we share your heavenly food,
and shine with your light
all the days of our life;
through Jesus Christ our Lord.

All   **Amen.**

Copyright Information

The Archbishops' Council of the Church of England and the other copyright owners and administrators of texts included in *Common Worship: Christian Initiation* have given permission for the use of their material in local reproductions on a non-commercial basis which comply with the conditions for reproductions for local use set out in the Archbishops' Council's booklet, *A Brief Guide to Liturgical Copyright.* This is available from:

www.commonworship.com

A reproduction which meets the conditions stated in that booklet may be made without an application for copyright permission or payment of a fee, but the following copyright acknowledgement must be included:

> *Common Worship: Christian Initiation*, material from which is included in this service, is copyright © The Archbishops' Council 2006.

Permission must be obtained in advance for any reproduction which does not comply with the conditions set out in *A Brief Guide to Liturgical Copyright.* Applications for permission should be addressed to:

The Copyright Administrator
The Archbishops' Council
Church House
Great Smith Street
London SW1P 3AZ
Telephone: 020 7898 1451
Fax: 020 7898 1449
Email: copyright@churchofengland.org